Kei

The True Friend

Dear William,

Thank you William for continuing to inspire so many of us in so many ways. This book was written in honor of your memory. I will always remember you as being a very bright student with a great sense of humor. We loved hearing your jokes and you were well liked by your classmates.

I vividly remember the time during recess when you told a bully to stop hurting another student. You showed courage and the kindness in your heart when you helped the child who was being bullied. We miss you everyday and we will always remember you!

Your Teacher and Friend
Kinota Braithwaite Classroom Teacher
Montessori School of Tokyo

Dedicated to the Memory of William Quin

Kei
The True Friend

Written By Kinota Braithwaite
Translated By Makiko Shimada

Kei had grown up in Canada. He loved the wintertime because he could play in the snow and make snowmen.

ケイはカナダで育った。雪遊びをしたり、雪だるまを作ったりすることのできる冬が好きだ。

On Sunday mornings he would wake up early and cook breakfast together with his Dad. Kei's favorite meal was buttermilk pancakes with maple syrup.

日曜の朝は早起きをして、父親と朝食を作る。メイプルシロップのかかったバターミルクのパンケーキはケイの大好物だ。

After having breakfast, Kei would go out on the pond to play ice hockey. He always had fun skating on the ice while passing the hockey puck back and forth to his friends.

朝食をすませると、ケイはアイスホッケーをしに池へ出かける。厚く張った氷の上を、たくさんの友達とパックを打ち合いながらスケートをするのはいつも楽しかった。

Kei's family was different from other Canadian families. His mother had been born in Japan and his father was African Canadian. That did not matter at all to Kei as he loved going ice fishing on the lake, sliding down hills on a toboggan and snowshoeing on the trails with his mom and dad.

ケイの家は、友達のカナダ人の家庭とは少し違っている。ケイの母親は日本人、父親はアフリカ系カナダ人なのだ。でも、そんな事はケイにとってはどうでもいいことで、凍てついた湖で穴釣りをしたり、そりに乗って雪の丘を一気にすべり降りたり、スノーシュー（かんじき）をはいて白い森の小道をハイキングしたり、両親と共に過ごす時間がケイは何よりも好きだった。

One day, Kei's grandpa in Japan called his mom.
Grandpa told her, "I am afraid I don't have good
news to share with you. The doctors have told me
that the cancer has spread."

ある日のこと、日本に住むケイの祖父から連絡があった。
「悪い知らせですまないんだが…
　ガンが進行していると医者に言われたんだよ」

In Japanese culture, it is the tradition that the oldest child takes care of their parents. Kei's mom and dad decided that they would move to Japan from Canada to take care of Grandpa.

長女であるケイの母親が自分の両親の面倒をみるのは、日本の文化ではごく当たり前のことだ。遠く離れて住む"日本のおじいちゃん"のために、ケイの両親は家族そろってカナダを離れ、日本に移り住む決心をした。

Kei started Jr. High school in Tokyo, Japan and he struggled to adjust to his new school. Often his classmates would make fun of him because he had trouble speaking Japanese. Everything was so different here in Japan and Kei felt all alone and wanted to return back to Canada.

こうしてケイの日本での生活が始まった。
東京にある新しい中学校に慣れるのは本当に大変だった。
日本語のほとんど話せないケイを、同級生が馬鹿にするのは
しょっちゅうだったし、日本での何もかもがそれまでの生活とは
違っていた。ひとりぼっちだな…カナダに帰りたいな…ケイはそう
思うようになっていった。

Grandpa saw that Kei was having a hard time adjusting to life in Japan. He told Kei that when he was a child, he had trained in the sport of Kendo. Kendo is the way of the sword, which comes from Japanese samurai warriors.

そんなケイの心の中は、おじいちゃんにはお見通しだった。
「ケイ、おじいちゃんが子供のころケンドウをやっていたのは知っているかい。ケンドウって『剣の道』って書くんだけど、もともとは日本の武士道から始まっているんだよ。」

Kendo can teach courage and develop the beauty of your spirit. It might be worth considering joining the Kendo club, as you will make friends there and learn about the traditional Japanese culture.

「だから、剣道は単なるスポーツじゃない。稽古をしながら武士の心構えを学んでいくものなんだ。そうして自分の精神を鍛えあげて、何ものにも負けない強い心を持つ自分を目指すんだよ。ケイ、剣道クラブに通ってみないかい。友達を作ったり、日本の文化に触れたりするいい機会になると思うんだがね」

Kendo training was difficult and Kei was shy at first but started to love practicing Kendo. He made many friends at the dojo and finally felt at home and accepted.

剣道の稽古は厳しかった。最初はなかなか馴染めなかったケイだが、次第に稽古に打ち込むようになった。夢中で稽古するうちに、道場では新しい友達がたくさんできた。気が付いたら、みんなと打ち解けていて、日本に来て、はじめて自分の居場所をみつけられたような気持ちになっていた。

A new girl came from England named Skye. She looked different from her classmates and they often ignored her or said mean things to her.

イギリスから転校生がやってきた。周囲とは顔立ちの違うスカイという名前の女の子。でも、スカイはクラスメイトから仲間外れにされたり意地悪を言われたりすることが多かった。そう、彼女の顔が『周りとは違う』というただそれだけの理由で。

Deep in his heart, Kei wanted to help Skye but was afraid of what the other students would say if he helped her. He was afraid they would bully him again too.

なんとかしなくちゃ、と心の奥底でケイは思った。と、同時にケイは考えた。もし、自分がスカイを助けようとしたら他の生徒は何と言うだろう。自分もまた以前のようにいじめられてしまうのではないだろうか…。

One day when Kei came home from school his parents looked very worried. They said, "Kei, we must go to the hospital. Your Grandpa is very sick now."

ある日、ケイが学校から帰ると、不安げな様子の両親が言った。「ケイ、病院へ急ごう。おじいちゃんの具合が悪いんだ」

At the hospital, Grandpa greeted Kei by asking, "How was your day?" Kei said it was not so good because some students were making fun of a new student named Skye. He said that he had wanted to help her by telling them to stop but was afraid they would start making fun of him too. Grandpa looked at Kei and said, "I am very weak now Kei, but in life we must not watch others being bullied. It is difficult I know but when you see someone being bullied then you must have the courage to try to help."

「学校はどうだい？」 病室のおじいちゃんはケイの顔を見るなりたずねた。「あんまり…よくないかな」 ケイは話し続けた。新しく来たスカイという名前の転校生が学校で馬鹿にされていること、その子を助けたいとは思うけれど、自分がまたいじめられるんじゃないかと怖くなって、友達に何も言えないでいること。すると、ケイの顔をじっと見つめて、おじいちゃんは言った。

「あのな、おじいちゃんは心も体もこんなに弱ってきているけれど、もし目の前で誰かがいじめにあっていたら、見て見ぬフリは絶対にしない。確かに難しいことだと思う。でも、ケイ、お前なら勇気を出して、その子を助けてあげられるはずだよ」

Kei saw Skye waiting outside the school and said, "I saw what happened and I am sorry that I did not help you when those kids were bullying you. When I first came to Japan, people made fun of me too. I joined the Kendo club and I made friends. Maybe you would like to join; we have practice at the dojo tomorrow."

スカイは校門の外で誰かを待っているみたいだった。ケイは思い切って声をかけた。
「ごめんな。君がいじめられているのを知っていて、今まで何もしようとしないで黙って見てた。僕も日本に来たばっかりの頃は、よく馬鹿にされていて…それで剣道クラブに入って、いろんな友達ができたんだ。もし良かったら、剣道始めてみない？　明日道場で練習があるんだけど。」

Skye said, "That sounds really nice Kei. I would love to join."

「ありがとう、ケイくん。私、剣道、やってみようかな」

Kei and Skye practiced Kendo every day and through the martial art of Kendo they both developed a sense of courage, confidence and respect for others.

それから、ケイとスカイは毎日剣道の稽古を続けた。剣道を通じて二人は武道の精神−立ち向かう勇気、自分を信じる心、そして他者への思いやりを学んでいった。

One day after Kendo practice, Skye said to Kei, "I was feeling so bad and all alone but now I am so happy to know that I have a good friend. Kei, thank you for helping me when I needed it the most. Kei you are a true friend."

ある日、稽古の後でスカイが言った。
「前はね、もう何もかもが嫌になって、自分はひとりぼっちだなって絶望していたの。でも、もうそうじゃない。私には友達がいるもの。ありがとう、ケイ。私が本当に困っているときに、あなたが助けてくれたの。ケイ、あなたこそが本当の友達よ。」

The End

www.ingramcontent.com/pod-product-compliance
Lightning Source LLC
LaVergne TN
LVHW070120180726
843515LV00011BA/2671